Walking with Grace
Revised

Walking with Grace
Revised

Tools for Implementing and Launching
a Congregational Respite Program

Robin Dill

WALKING WITH GRACE REVISED
TOOLS FOR IMPLEMENTING AND LAUNCHING A CONGREGATIONAL RESPITE PROGRAM

iUniverse books may be ordered through booksellers or by contacting:

iUniverse
1663 Liberty Drive
Bloomington, IN 47403
www.iuniverse.com
1-800-Authors (1-800-288-4677)

Because of the dynamic nature of the Internet, any web addresses or links contained in this book may have changed since publication and may no longer be valid. The views expressed in this work are solely those of the author and do not necessarily reflect the views of the publisher, and the publisher hereby disclaims any responsibility for them.

Any people depicted in stock imagery provided by Thinkstock are models, and such images are being used for illustrative purposes only.
Certain stock imagery © Thinkstock.

ISBN: 978-1-5320-1189-4 (sc)
ISBN: 978-1-5320-1190-0 (e)

Print information available on the last page.

iUniverse rev. date: 12/18/2016

The Caregiver

As I watch you fall into memories
Of oh-so long ago...
My face becomes a stranger-
One you no longer know.

Often there are good days and
We sit and talk as friends.
My loneliness and bitterness
Are like they'd never been.

But all too soon you turn away-
Push aside my caring hands...
I'm left to love for the both of us-
Making futile, empty plans.

So each morning as I talk with God,
And we share our love for you...
He gives me strength as I speak your name
And I pray you'll know me too.

Jane Johnson

Dedication

Eleven years have passed since I was hired to implement, launch, and direct a day program for adults dealing with memory loss. When I wrote *Walking with Grace* in 2008-2009, I felt I had enough knowledge to assist churches in their journey to vision and to consider respite for their congregation. Seven more years of experience have propelled me to update this manual. I echo what I wrote in 2008: much prayer, time, thought, and encouragement has gone into writing this manual. It is amazing to think how God uses experiences in our daily lives to create an opportunity for ministry. If my mom had not had brain cancer that went into dementia, I am not sure I would be doing what I am doing. However, through that experience, working as a volunteer in Pastoral Care in two Atlanta hospitals, being a Stephen Minister, and a thousand other experiences and people caused me to apply for the job to implement, launch, and direct an Older Adult Day program at First United Methodist Church in Lawrenceville, Georgia. I celebrate the longevity of this ministry under the direction and empowerment of the Holy Spirit, as well as the hard work of my assistant Cindy Leake and our amazing volunteers!

My dream is that "The Church" will see clearly its role in health care for the family. The church has the unique opportunity to provide care to adults in a loving compassionate way. Through utilizing members' spiritual gifts, talents, resources, and energy a vibrant and successful program can be birthed and run.

It is to all those people at Grace Arbor that I dedicate this manual. To the volunteers and my assistant director, Cindy Leake, who work tirelessly to love and support our participants I give you thanks! You all have taught me so much! To the caregivers of these precious participants who are putting their lives on hold and caring 24/7, I am humbly grateful to walk with you on this journey. To the incredible participants of Grace Arbor who bring me joy, laughter, love, acceptance, and learning, I give you my profound appreciation!

I dedicate this manual also to my family. They are the ones who heard a thousand stories, offered up prayer, and care to me when I needed it. They were the ones who said to me, "Yes, you can do it!" They have been the ones who have believed in me even when I didn't! Thank you!

Soli Deo Gloria!

Robin Dill
Fall 2016

Introduction

Whether you are considering starting a congregational respite program or have already made the commitment to begin one, I hope and pray this manual will aid you in exploring, developing, and launching a ministry at your church that targets memory-impaired older adults. Respite ministry can have a tremendous impact on a church and their community both within and outside their doors. As a director in her twelfth year of respite ministry, I can confirm and affirm the work our ministry does on a daily basis within Gwinnett County and beyond. Jesus reminds us that whatever we do to the least we do unto Him. Respite ministries experience this over and over!

Our ministry, Grace Arbor, was the vision of a group of church members who had the need for respite care for their memory-impaired loved ones. It took the church over four years of persistent inquiry and planning before they were ready to hire someone to develop this program, launch, and then direct it.

It was during this time that God was preparing me for this work. After a move from one state to another, I took the training to become a Stephen Minister and served in two hospitals in the Atlanta area on their pastoral care teams. My mom developed brain cancer during this time. Dementia became part of my personal life experience. I saw first-hand how much respite care impacted my dad. Then my husband experienced cancer and God taught me about being a caregiver. So many life experiences prepared me for the ministry of Grace Arbor; God orchestrated them all for my good and His glory. After mom's death and my husband's recovery, I felt restlessness in my spirit, and I knew God was getting me ready for a new ministry. When I saw the ad in the paper about the church starting a day program, it took the encouragement of my family to answer it. For me this is where Proverbs 3:5-6 came to life: "***Trust in the Lord with all your heart and lean not on your own understanding; in all your ways acknowledge Him, and He will make your paths straight."*** I committed the plan of an older adult program, a congregational respite program to Him. I asked Him to use me and provide for all the needs of this program. Time and again, He directed me to needed resources even to how we came to name this program Grace Arbor. This ministry and my service continue to be His work and to His glory!

My prayer for you is that you will take the time to carefully read through the chapters. As you read them keep a pencil and notebook handy to jot down ideas and needs you think of as the Holy Spirit prompts you. I have tried to think of as many details I could to aid you in creating a quality, Spirit-filled program that will minister to families in crisis that would impact memory-impaired older adults. Check out the resource guide at the end of the book for aids to help you with ideas, equipment, and support.

Besides praying as I prepared to lead this program, I read as many resources as I could to help me in preparing to lead this ministry. Take advantage of trainings offered by your local chapter of the Alzheimer's Association. Take training through Teepa Snow and use her videos as you train your staff. Check out local colleges in your area for any courses that you might take, including auditing courses to offer you further equipping. Become trained through the Center for Applied Research in Dementia by Dr. Cameron Camp. Research the Internet for any training programs coming your way through your local senior services or Division of Aging. Take time to visit other programs offering respite to get ideas and encouragement. Once you are up and running, form a network with other directors to keep your ideas fresh. Keep seeking and the Lord will overwhelm you with the resources to aid you in your planning, implementing, and running of your program.

Getting Started

Apple Pie Day

Every year we celebrate Apple Pie Day. We make 35 apple pies from scratch which we use for our pastor appreciation luncheon and other times during the year. This is an opportunity to combine a service project with memories our participants have of their times in the kitchen.

Getting Started

Starting a Congregational Respite program will be one of the greatest spiritual adventures a church can undertake to do. The opportunities to impact families in a time of crisis are monumental, as well as the opportunities to provide the way for church and community members to utilize their gifts and talents! Memory impairment in older adults is on the increase.

Statistics from the 2016 Alzheimer's Association are staggering. Right now over 5 million people have Alzheimer's disease. Alzheimer's disease is the sixth leading cause of death in the United States. One in three seniors dies with Alzheimer's disease or another dementia. In 2015, more than 15 million caregivers provided an estimated 18.1 billion hours of unpaid care. These are statistics that the church needs to pay attention to as their congregations are affected by this. This population needs support and assistance. I believe that it can be the church's mission to accomplish this.

The greatest work a church can do as it considers opening a Congregational Respite program is to pray. Our Lord and Savior promised the Holy Spirit to all who seek Him. Under His direction you will be able to develop an amazing fruit-bearing ministry; apart from Him, you won't. As you begin, I would encourage a team of people who have a heart for this ministry to pray and seek God for a period of time; i.e. take a month to write down what the Lord might reveal to each as they pray. After the time is up, gather together and have each person share what the Lord has shown to them. I believe you will then have the beginnings of your ministry.

I would seek wise counsel. Talk to people in the community about needs. Talk to doctors, to county senior organizations, and to the local chapter of tAlzheimer's Association about the numbers of calls they are getting for help. As you poll Sunday school classes in the various churches, target not only older adult classes, but mid-age classes as well. They, too, might be the caregivers to aging parents or grandparents. The needs in your church and community will make themselves known.

As you seek wise counsel you will need to prepare a financial plan to pay for this ministry. Will this come about as a "line item" in the church budget? Perhaps a gift or memorial might be the financial springboard to get it going. You might consider applying for a grant. Whatever route you choose, you will need money in hand to purchase equipment, to modify an existing space or to build a new space to house this ministry, and to pay salaries for the staff that will be hired to implement, launch, and direct this program.

Another important component to this process is researching your state and local laws concerning respite programs. Are programs like these licensed by the state in which your church is located? If not, what are the guidelines, rules, and regulations you must follow in order **not** to be licensed? In the state of Georgia a group of congregational Respite program directors worked diligently with state legislators to prevent these programs from being licensed.

As you go through this process, contact existing programs in other communities, as well as the Alzheimer's Association for help with training and "shadowing." These visits and training will prove invaluable as you plan this ministry for your church. These people will be able to assist you with any guidelines that your state might require for a respite program. Your Area Agency on Aging will be able to answer questions for you.

The more you plan on the front end, the "surprises" will occur after you are well on your way to starting your program. Prayer, seeking wise counsel, putting together a financial plan, and looking into the state laws will aid you in putting together a plan. Shadowing existing programs and seeking support from the Alzheimer's Association will help to fine tune that plan. Now you are ready to fine tune even further by looking at your space, purchasing equipment and supplies, and begin to get your paperwork in order.

Equipment and Supplies

Volunteer Appreciation Luncheon

Equipment and Supplies

The term **equipment** encompasses non-consumable items that are used on a daily basis. This will include chairs, tables, coffeepots, dishes, etc. An assessment of what your church presently has in the way of equipment will be helpful in reducing this component of your startup budget. Asking church members for donations will also be helpful. Don't be afraid to refuse any item that will not fit your needs. If you don't need an item, it is better to say *no* than to take up storage space with something you won't use.

The following is a list of necessary items. From my experience, each item on this list will help you as you creatively plan your program. Some things, such as mixers or blenders, will not be needed until you do a cooking project; others you will need right away. The Internet is a valuable tool to use as you search for these items. Comparison shop! Don't be afraid to ask for discounts or donations from a company. Asking for a discount price because you are starting a respite ministry might generate some additional equipment.

Necessary Equipment

1. Sturdy Arm Chairs that can be stacked for storage
2. Tables for eating and doing activities
3. Dishes: mugs, glasses, plates (luncheon and dessert), bowls, silverware, pitchers for drinks, cream and sugar containers, bowls, casseroles, and serving utensils for lunch and cooking projects, cookie sheets. [Note: If you have a working kitchen in your church being used for Wednesday night dinners, some of these items may possibly be borrowed on a regular basis.]
4. Two 36-cup coffee pots: one for coffee and one for hot water for tea and hot chocolate
5. Microwave for heating and cooking projects
6. Toaster oven or full-size oven
7. Electric mixer
8. Blender
9. Cloth tablecloths (solid or checked)
10. Sing-along books, large print
11. Hymnals, large print
12. Communion dishes/cloth for table
13. Storage Units:cupboards with counter tops
14. Working sink with running hot and cold water
15. Cloth hand towels; wash rags
16. Nametags: clear plastic holder with clip not pin
17. Name place cards for the table with holders
18. Wipeable placemats
19. Clothes' protectors for lunchtime
20. Decorating items-quilts for the walls, pictures, flower vases, silk flower arrangements for the tables when fresh flowers aren't available, seasonal décor, Christmas tree with lights built in, unbreakable ornaments.
21. Aprons for crafts/plastic gloves
22. CD player with Blue Tooth
23. Laptop projector and screen
24. Exercise Equipment: balls-yoga, small balls, nerf balls, bands,1# beans, plastic basketball goal, net for balloon volleyball, balloons, bean bags
25. White board and markers/eraser for daily schedule
26. First Aid Kit
27. Telephone
28. File cabinet
29. Computer w/printer
30. Yearly calendar
31. Accordion file with manila folders for participant records

32. Digital camera
33. Carrying baskets
34. Computer Financial Program to do billing
35. Extra wheelchairs and walkers
36. Extra sweaters or sweatshirts
37. Three drawer carts for ladies' and men's bathrooms for supplies-gloves, Depends, wipes, plastic bags, etc.
38. Piano or keyboard
39. Sleeping bag or cot for emergencies

Chairs are one of the most important pieces of equipment you will purchase. When shopping for chairs look for chairs that have arms that can be stacked and wiped clean and sanitized. When we launched Grace Arbor, we used Grsiflex Pacific Fanback chairs. These were high-grade plastic chairs with high backs that could be stacked. Over the years, we purchased cloth cushions that we used in the chairs. When a sizeable donation came in last year, we researched vinyl chairs and used Dallas Midwest Company to supply healthcare-grade vinyl-covered armchairs. These chairs came in a variety of colors. We decided on a black chair with royal blue vinyl. We have been very pleased with both the color choice and the style.

When I started Grace Arbor, we had bulky old tables. We made do with these until the ministry could afford to purchase replacements. I have since replaced these tables with the white plastic ones you can buy at the different discount stores. They come in various sizes. We use 8-foot, 4-foot, and round tables in the program. The 4-foot table makes a nice "communion" table when draped with a white cloth. The fact that they are plastic makes them easy to move and wipe clean after projects. They are stackable as well for ease in storage.

Dishes were an important investment as I wanted to create a friendly atmosphere of "home" that would spark fellowship and conversation. We do not eat on paper plates with plastic utensils at home nor do we drink from Styrofoam cups. I considered safety a big factor, especially with cups and mugs. Were they easily tipped? Were they too heavy for older arthritic hands to pick up? Were they cost-effective? Were they environmentally friendly? Could they be easily cleaned and sanitized? I have bought white mugs, plates and bowls. Food can easily be seen on white. I offer words of caution, however; don't put a white plate, mug, or bowl on a white placemat. White on white or any of the same color on the same color can be "lost" visually to someone with memory impairment. If you have someone who has Parkinson's disease or is visually impaired, research alternative utensils and dishes. We had a local potter create some double-handled bowls.

I decided cloth tablecloths were better than vinyl. They were tactilely more appealing and would last longer. Additionally, they added to that homey atmosphere. I have found the less busy the pattern the better the impact on the table. (See example in picture.) I have several colors that can be used for different seasons. For example, red and white check or solid red can be used in February, July, and December and on Memorial Day and Veterans Day. I have laminated construction paper for placemats. Some are plain but most are in designs that a volunteer created. These are seasonal with matching name place cards. My name card holders are metal and were purchased through a restaurant supply company.

I use colorful seasonal cocktail napkins that go with placemats for morning snack, adding again to that homey atmosphere. Anything that is visually appealing is important. I may just use solid colored or find print ones. *One way to get these is to advertise in the bulletin for members to donate cocktail napkins!* You will be amazed at the results. I use white paper napkins for lunch with the exception of birthdays and holidays.

I am not a fan of silk flowers; however, they are useful on the lunch and snack table if fresh ones are not available. Ask anyone in the church during flower growing season if they would bring flowers on a weekly basis for your tables. You can also decorate tables with seasonal fruit and vegetables as well. Anything that will stimulate and start conversation is great!

My hymnal over the years had been a 1and 1/2 inch binder with large-print music inserted in plastic sleeves. Recently we have upgraded to an all word, large-print hymnal called *Hymns We Love to Sing.* This spiral bound lightweight book is available through Wood Lake Publishing. There is a music and word book available for your piano accompanist.

Sing-along books are 1 and 1/2 inch binders with plastic sleeves. In the sleeves are the words in large print-Arial 20-point font or larger. Page numbers are on the bottom left hand side. I have binders with just Christmas music-both sacred and secular. The binders are 1 and 1/2 inches so they won't be too heavy.

Nametags and place cards at the table are important for several reasons. Memory-impaired adults have a hard time remembering names. Until you and your volunteers get to know everyone well, *you will forget their names, too!* Nametags solve that dilemma. Reusable nametags that clip on work well. On the nametag, print the participants name in a large Arial font in a color that is different from that of your volunteers! I use purple for participants and black for volunteers. These colors are close enough to distinguish between but not glaringly obvious that they are different. We are careful to address this idea of similarity to make the participants feel *part* of

the ministry–actively involved–not set apart because they are being cared for in your program. Your nametags will serve as a safety feature as well. Somewhere on the tag–front or back–identify your program name in case a participant wanders off and is found by someone. I laminate my tags with my business card on the back, with the church's phone number and address on it. Your nametags can also have identifying marks that tell your volunteers that a person is a diabetic. We use a red heart to identify our diabetics.

Place cards at the table will allow for targeted placement of your participants. You will be able to control where they sit and by whom. I try to mix volunteers in between participants as much as possible to keep the conversation flowing. Volunteer placement can aid in personality conflicts between participants. If a participant needs some assistance at meal time, a well-placed volunteer can be very helpful. On the place card, as on the nametag, a red heart is used to identify someone who is a diabetic.

Supplies

Supplies are the consumable things used on a daily, weekly, or monthly basis. These will be replaced as needed basis. These things could be identified for your church's congregation as items to be donated. Suggest when someone shops could they pick up a box of decaf tea or hot chocolate. You will need to be specific about brand names and quantities!

1. Decaffeinated Coffee, Decaffeinated Tea bags-both individual and family size, hot chocolate-plain, no sugar added, and diet, lemonade (sugar free).
2. Sugar, Splenda, whole milk, whipped cream (for hot chocolate)
3. Paper products: paper plates for crafts as well as desserts or snacks where you don't want to use china; paper towels, napkins, both cocktail and luncheon, and paper towels
4. Clear plastic service gloves for serving food and doing crafts
5. Condiments for meals and snacks
6. Sanitizing wipes (whatever is on sale)
7. Dishwashing detergent/sponges
8. Lysol or other disinfecting spray
9. Depends disposable undergarments, pads
10. Gloves-latex or non-latex-exam gloves for emergencie

Staffing

Robin Dill and Cindy Leake during Vacation Bible School Week

Kellsey Kloker, Robin Dill, and David Pianka
College Student Volunteer Recognition

Staffing

In this section I will discuss staff, both paid and volunteer. Without a staff that is godly, Spirit-empowered, and with a heart for this kind of ministry, you will fail. Your staff is vital to this ministry on many levels. It is your staff who will be assisting you in the ministry to your participants and programming functions. They will be your prayer partners, advocates, servants and advertisers. If they have a heart for this ministry and feel validated and appreciated, they will do just about anything for you because they believe in what they do. I can't say enough about how important the paid and volunteer staff is!

As I began to plan Grace Arbor I did several things to advertise the need for help. At that time I was the only paid staff. I knew that I needed a group of people who would commit to one day or part of a day on a weekly basis. I also needed people who would be willing to substitute for the regular volunteers. The first thing I did was to pray. I asked the Lord to move in the hearts of those who had hearts for this type of ministry. I prayed for volunteers who loved older people and who weren't afraid of interacting with people who are memory-impaired.

After I prayed I began to advertise in our church's bulletin and monthly newsletter. I tried to include both eye-catching and heart-catching ads about the needs of this ministry. Then I began to meet people and to share personally about this ministry. I spoke during church services and visited Sunday school classes. I even put an ad in our *Parent Morning Out* and Preschool's newsletters, hoping some moms who had time on their hands might be willing to help. I asked around, and people gave me names of people I personally contacted.

As I interviewed each potential "staff" member I asked them to share with me why they wanted to volunteer and what experiences they had had with people with memory impairment. Most of my volunteers have had a family member, a neighbor, or a friend who suffered with dementia. If someone were too "close" to the situation, I asked that they wait or serve in another way that didn't involve immediate contact with persons with dementia. I learned early on that these questions are important. I had recruited a volunteer who was helping with food because her parents had recently died from dementia. I felt as though she didn't need to be in too close contact with our participants. The situation went from bad to worse, and we both realized at about the same time that she had not given herself sufficient time to grieve. She dropped out of the staff pool at about the time I was going to ask her to leave.

We are committed to providing the best quality care we can for our caregivers. This is why we conduct a background check on all staff, both paid and volunteer. Taking this step has been an added cost to our budget, but it has been well worth it in the confidence we portray to our caregivers. Depending on your state's requirements, you may require a TB test for all staff. This is another added assurance for caregivers.

God is so faithful. At the time when we needed volunteers, He assembled a mighty group of men and women who were committed to serving in the areas of their gifts and talents. My promise to them was that I would provide the training to equip them to do what I asked them to do. I have kept that commitment by having quarterly trainings to empower each volunteer with knowledge about behaviors, elder abuse, and safety issues. I asked our local chapter of the Alzheimer's Association to assist in those trainings initially until I felt comfortable enough to do them on my own.

As our program has grown, we have added paid staff. I have an (almost) fulltime Assistant Director and a part-time cook who handles meals and snacks. Each addition has brought blessings and challenges. The blessings are sharing in the ministry and its precious people we serve. The challenges are to train and support paid staff while directing a fulltime ministry that serves caregivers, participants, and volunteers. I juggle many balls, and without the Holy Spirit and a loving, supportive family I would be failing at what I do.

As I recruited paid staff, the same philosophy applied: I looked for people who have a heart for this ministry and who have experience working with memory-impaired older adults. This work is not for everyone.

When I interviewed for my Assistant Director's job, I looked for high-energy, social people who were qualified in certain ways. It was not a quick work, and I interviewed many people. My requirement before I hire either volunteers or staff is that they come and spend a day at Grace Arbor. You learn a lot about people as you observe them in action. For the paid staff, I might have them spend a week shadowing me. It is necessary for people to experience this type of ministry firsthand. Many may have a preconceived idea of what it looks like. Unless they are there, hands-on, they will never know what it is really like to work in that environment.

My assistant director must be certified in Alzheimer's care. This is a 22-hour program offered by the Alzheimer's Association. The daily workshops cover a lot of ground. This program is a tool that is important in the overall plan of the ministry. My assistant director must also be CPR-and First Aid-trained. Both of these trainings will prepare him or her to step into my shoes if I have to be out for any reason. I would try to set my schedule to not be away during the first three months of training. As he or she gains confidence, I will gradually let him or her be "in charge" while I am present. This

helps me to share expectations after the day is over, affirming and guiding him or her to that place of confidence.

As I began to interview people for the Assistant Director's job, I heard a spot on the radio about singer Wayne Newton. He was being interviewed about some of the people on his show and how talented they were. The interviewer asked him if he was worried that someone would get so good, that he, Wayne Newton, would be out of a job.

Mr. Newton replied that he felt it was his job to support and help his singers become the very best they could be, even if he risked losing them. When I heard that, I thought **That is what I want to do!** I want to help people achieve to the greatest of their potential. If I can do that, I have done my best.

A couple of "out of the box" ideas in staffing have proved to be great blessings. We have opened the doors to teenagers wanting to volunteer. We have seen God do amazing ministry in and through these teenagers who grew into college students! We have allowed a few folks who needed community service hours to serve at Grace Arbor. These opportunities proved to be part of their healing for those folks. Don't be afraid to try someone. It may be one of the biggest blessings you might be a part of!

Training

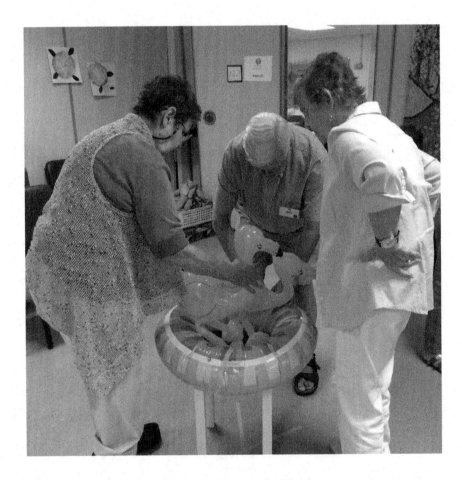

Summer Group Activity
A group of participants and volunteers had to create this game using a pool ring, two plastic flamingos, small rings to toss, and a roll of masking tape.

Training

As I mentioned in the previous section, I made a covenant with my volunteers concerning training. It is my job as director to help my staff, both volunteer and paid, to be the best they can be as they serve these precious participants. The more people are educated and gain knowledge concerning a particular subject, the better able they are to be prepared to apply that knowledge to any given situation. The more my staff knows about dementia–its behaviors, triggers that cause behavior, and how to react in certain situations-the better our program will run. Instead of me rushing to put out fires, my staff will be anticipating them before they get started with their loving knowledge, which translates into caring behavior. I can't say enough about the importance of good training.

One aspect of training I find extremely helpful in working with people with dementia is for our staff to be able to role play. As we learn about a behavior and its triggers, we will role play what that might look like. Each day has so many examples, as well. I will try to bring up examples of situations they have experienced, and we will brainstorm how to handle them: what might work and what won't normally work. Spot training is also very effective. If a challenging situation presents itself, it is an opportunity for a learning experience. At the end of the day and the subsequent days, I will cover with all volunteers what happened, how it was handled, and what we could have done differently. I engage my volunteers for their opinions, but I am ultimately the decision maker.

Here are some ideas from past trainings I have done that will equip you as you start and sustain your program:

1. General Overview of Dementia
2. Behaviors–What to Expect
3. Behavioral Triggers–the Hows and Whys and How to Respond
4. Elder Abuse
5. Participant's Rights
6. Brief Overview of Montessori Method
7. Safety: Universal Precautions
8. CPR/ First Aid training
9. Role Playing
10. Teepa Snow videos–available through her website
11. Book Studies: *No Act of Love is Ever Wasted* by Jane Thibaut and Richard Morgan; *The Four Things that Matter Most* by Dr. Ira Byock
12. Art therapy trainings–the "how to" create a setting and implement an art project for people with dementia

Volunteers Training

Role Playing

The following situations can be used in a training class where volunteers pair up, discuss the scenario and their solution, and then discuss as a group. Each situation can be adapted to actual situations you have dealt with in your program.

Situation 1:

You are sitting in the chair circle–morning or afternoon group time, and the participant next to you suddenly gets up and walks to the door. What will you do?

Situation 2:

You are sitting next to someone at the lunch table who is not eating at all. What are you going to do?

Situation 3:

You are sitting at the lunch table and the director gives the invitation to come and do an activity and the participant next to you says, "I don't want to do that." What are you going to do?

Situation 4:

You are sitting in group and two participants sitting near you get into a verbal sparring match. What are you going to do?

Situation 5:

As you are sitting in group you notice one of the participants become glassy-eyed and rigid in body posturing. What are you going to do?

Situation 6:

You are in the bathroom with a participant and she bangs her elbow on the stall door and it begins to bleed. What are you going to do?

Situation 7:

The director is leading devotional and the participant next to you is talking to another participant rather than paying attention. What are you going to do?

Situation 8:

You and a participant are having a conversation about life and the participant shares an elaborate story about his or her past. What are you going to do?

Paperwork, i.e., Forms and Documents

Sing along Time with Guests

Paperwork, I.E. Forms, and Documents

Paperwork, i.e. forms and documents, are the record of what you do on a daily basis. The more organized you can be in your paperwork, the easier your job will be as you go through your day. As I go through this section, I will give examples of the forms I use. You will need to change them to fit your specific needs. I will split this into several sections that will explain the type of form, why you need it, and what it does for you in your recordkeeping.

1. **Potential Participant Folder with documents**
   a. Letter from Pastor
   b. Bylaws and Procedures
   c. Medical Release
   d. Emergency Release
   e. Photo and Field Trip Release
   f. Participant Information Sheets
   g. Business Card with Grace Arbor's contact information
   h. Brochure about Grace Arbor
   i. Current newsletter

2. **Participant File*** *Keep this in Program Room at all times in Accordion File***
   a. Medical Release
   b. TB Results
   c. Emergency Release
   d. Photo and Field Trip Release
   e. Participant Information Sheets
   f. Current Photo
   g. Drug information Sheet if separate from info sheet
   h. DNR, living will, and advanced directives if hospice patient

3. **Volunteer Folder with documents**
   a. Reducing the Risk Background check
   b. Information Sheet w/emergency contact
   c. Covenant

4. **Attendance Roll**
5. **Telephone Call Sheet**

6. **Safety Forms**
   a. Fire Drill Report
   b. Participant Accident Form
   c. Volunteer Accident Form

7. **Calendar**
8. **Caregiver Monthly Newsletter**
9. **Volunteer Monthly Newsletter**
10. **911 Call Sheet**
11. **Emergency Activity Folder**
12. **Participant Notebook**
13. **Brochure and Business Cards**

1. Potential Participant Folder with documents:

This is what I hand to a caregiver after we have determined together their loved one will be a part of the Grace Arbor ministry. I use a two-pocket folder so that forms can be on one side and caregiver information on the other side.

It was decided that a *letter from our pastor* was an added assurance to the caregiver that our church and our pastor are behind this ministry 100%.

The most time-consuming piece of paper for you will be the creation of your *Bylaws and Policies and Procedures sheets*. These will give the caregiver the assurance that you have policies and procedures in place for the safety of their loved one. These documents will be developed as you and your committee decide what to do when you take someone from "intake" to leaving the program permanently. These lay out the structure of your program and how you will do what you say you will do.

The *medical release form* is one the caregiver gives to the doctor to fill out to say that this potential participant is physically able to participate in our program.

The *emergency release form* will give us the permission to care for and get care for this participant in the event of an emergency. This directs the ambulance to the hospital of choice in case we have to call 911. I give the ambulance driver a copy of their drug information sheet.

The *photo and field trip release forms* are self-explanatory. If you take pictures or have an event printed in the newspaper, this is nice to have on hand. However, if you are filmed by an outside entity, you will be asked to have a release on every person filmed.

The *information sheet* includes vital questions about this person's past, former life prior to memory loss, and what they can do now. This also has a place for contact info. I can't stress enough to get plenty of phone numbers in case of an emergency.

It is just as important for the caregiver to be able to reach me. I put two numbers on my *business card*-the church's number and the cell# to reach Grace Arbor. If you have two numbers, you might include them as well. I would hesitate to put my personal cell number on that business card due to privacy concerns.

I include a *brochure* in this folder. It briefly spells out our program and the fees. This is easier to read through than the policy and procedures. It is also there to be passed on to someone else, should there be other interest in our program.

A *monthly newsletter* contains current information and that month's schedule of activities.

2.Participant File* *Keep this in Program Room at all times in Accordion File**

I keep my accordion file with all my current participant folders with me at all times during the operating day of Grace Arbor. If we have a fire drill, it goes outside with me. I guard this with my life because it contains all the forms the participant's caregiver filled out. In addition to the completed forms they filled out, I keep their current *TB test results*, a *current photo* which I take, and any additional information the family might give me. For those in hospice care, I have the *DNR, living will, and advanced directives*. **Current prescriptions lists** may be found in this file as well. I lock this file up each night.

3. Volunteer Folder with documents

Our church has a policy which I think should pertain to any care-giving ministry. It is that all care-giving ministry volunteers must have a background check. We use the local police department. There is a fee for this, but it is well worth it in the long run. My volunteers also fill out a covenant in which they agree to certain things and I agree to certain things. They then sign and date this.

4. Attendance Roll

This sheet is set up to keep track of daily attendance of participants as well as serve as a financial sheet at the end of the month. I document the number of meals served to participants, volunteers and, staff.

5. Telephone Call Sheet

I use this sheet to take down information from phone calls concerning interest in our ministry. I will keep this in a folder to refer to if the caregiver isn't yet ready to visit. When I receive the next call from that caregiver, I have additional information to use in talking with him or her. This also a great way to track the number of calls you receive in a month.

6. Safety Forms

Safety forms need to be on hand at all times. **Fire drills** need to be documented. These should be done at least quarterly on different days with different volunteers present. These drills help prepare your program staff in case of a real emergency. Tornado drills would be extremely important, especially if you live in Tornado Alley.

Accident forms must be completed every time there is an incident requiring more than minor care (e.g., bumping thin skin which would call for cleansing and a Band-Aid versus a fall that might require more attention.) These forms should be filled out when this happens to anyone in the program area. These forms must be signed by the caregiver as documentation that they have been made aware of an accident and what kind of care was given. These signed forms need to be retained in the participant's folder as part of their permanent record. *Volunteer accidents* should also be documented.

7. Calendar

A notebook type of calendar will be extremely beneficial to you in all areas of your work as director of your program. I use an 18-month calendar which allows caregivers and volunteers to "sign out" when they aren't coming to Grace Arbor. I plan my attendance for the week in my calendar and then check it against true attendance. This helps me plan for additional volunteers and meals. I record meetings and anything else I need to keep track of by date. It is helpful if all staff members have one and then you can compare notes frequently to stay on track as a team.

I keep another type of a calendar for my activities and I use it for monthly planning. I actually download it from Outlook on my computer and print it on 11x17 inch paper. I keep a copy of this in my file cabinet under that particular month's folder. I keep files on different seasonal activities adjacent to these monthly folders so they are easily referred to as needed for planning.

8. Caregiver Monthly Newsletter

Every month I create a newsletter for both my caregivers and volunteers. I give this newsletter out in advance. In it I include a schedule of special activities we will do for that month. I might highlight special clothing needs pertaining to that activity. For example, if we are painting birdhouses on a certain day, I will ask them to wear old clothes. The challenge will be whether the caregiver keeps the calendar and refers to it frequently during the month. I communicate support group meetings and any information that needs to be relayed in the newsletters, and I list birthdays for that month.

9. Volunteer Monthly Newsletter

As in the caregiver newsletter, I include a schedule of specific events happening during the month, including birthdays. I will communicate any issues that might have come up during the past month to help in their ongoing training. Both the volunteer and the caregiver newsletters are important documents. I keep them in a file on my computer.

10. 911 Call Sheet

This is a set of instructions that anyone can use when calling 911 for our program. It contains our address and phone number and specific directions to our program room. In an emergency situation, volunteers may not be able to think as clearly as they would under normal circumstances. This is an aid to give them the support they need in a crisis. I have this posted in several areas: near the bathrooms and in other parts of our program room.

11. Emergency Activity Folder

This folder is vitally important to those who are assisting you in your program. If there is an emergency, this folder will equip a volunteer to do an activity with the remaining participants while the director and emergency personnel render aid. This folder should be easily accessible and full of different ideas depending on the time of day and the area of the room in which the crisis has occurred.

12. Participant Notebook

This is a binder which contains a sheet on each active participant in your program. Each sheet should include a picture and general information about this person. This binder helps volunteers become familiar with new participants. This takes time to keep current, but it is invaluable! It assists volunteers by listing pertinent information about each participant to aid them in conversation topics. For example, "Sue," a new participant was a WWII pilot who flew in active duty. As a volunteer, I can generate

conversation topics around those experiences, also engaging others who may also have served in WWII.

13. Brochure and Business Cards

Nothing speaks "professional" like a well-designed brochure and business cards. Your brochure could be the first impression a stranger will have as they learn about your program. A brochure should contain this pertinent information:

1. Your mission statement
2. The program's daily schedule
3. Activities–the particulars
4. Contact information for additional questions.

GRACE ARBOR
The Congregational Respite Program of
First United Methodist Church of Lawrenceville

Application Form

Full Name: _____ Date: _____ Fee Paid: _____

Address:_____

Male____ Female____ Birthday_____ Marital Status M__ S__ D__ Widow/er____

Presently lives with_____

How did you hear about our program? _____

EMERGENCY INFORMATION:

Doctor's Name, Address, Phone#:_____

Hospital Preference: _____

ALLERGIC TO: _____

List All Physical Problems, including mental health and communicable diseases:

_____

List Any Dietary or Physical Restrictions: _____

_____

List Medications/Dosage: _____

_____

CAREGIVER CONTACT INFORMATION:

Caregiver's Name: _____ Relationship_____

Address if different from participant: _____ Home Phone#_____

Cell Phone #_____ Work Phone #: _____

E-mail Address: _____

Alternate Contact Person: _____ Relationship_____

Address_____

Home Phone #_____ Work Phone #_____Cell Phone#_____

Use back for any additional information we may need to know to aid in the participant's care

_____ I have received and read a copy of the policies and procedures of GRACE ARBOR.

GRACE ARBOR

Interest Profile

Name: _____ Date: _____

Name Participant likes to be called: _____

Family History (marital history, number and names of children, where they live and other important relationships): _____

_____

_____

Friends/Pets:_____

_____

Childhood History (Place of birth, info on parents, nationality, languages spoken, experiences, past-times):

_____

_____

_____

Education/Former Occupations (Years of work, what they enjoyed):

_____

_____

Previous interests, Awards, Volunteer Activities: _____

_____

Current Interests and Hobbies: _____

_____

Musical Tastes (Play instrument? Sing? What music do they enjoy?):

_____

Clubs/Organizations: _____

Religious Preference: _____

Social Interaction (Enjoy large social functions? Small groups? Alone?):

_____

Comments: _____

_____

_____

_____

STATEMENT OF MEDICAL CONDITION

Dear Physician:

This patient has applied to attend **Grace Arbor, the Congregational Respite Program of First United Methodist Church.** Please certify that he/she is free of communicable diseases and has had the necessary and appropriate immunizations.

Name_____Birthdate_____

Address_____City/StateZip_____

Diagnosis_____

Date of last: Flu shot_____ Pneumonia vaccine_____

Tetanus Toxoid_____

TB test_____ Results were positive _____negative_____

Allergies: _____

Please circle the recommended diet for this patient:

      Regular   Low Salt   Low Cholesterol   Diabetic/low calorie

      Other_____

Special considerations/precautions/comments:_____

_____

I certify that the above-named patient is free of communicable diseases and recommend his/her participation in the Grace Arbor Congregational Respite Program.

Signature_____Date_____

Address_____

GRACE ARBOR

Consent for Emergency Medical Care

As a participant in the Grace Arbor Congregational Respite Program of First United Methodist Church of Lawrenceville, I hereby give permission to staff (paid and volunteers) to provide direct minor emergency care for minor emergencies or to access 911 emergency medical services as deemed necessary. I hereby give my full and unconditional approval for said staff to secure emergency medical care.

Any resultant bill will be the responsibility of the participant and /or caregiver/ guardian. Said individual(s) will be responsible for filing any and all medical insurance claims.

In the event a medical situation is not an emergency, staff may request that a doctor see the participant. It is understood that the participant cannot return to the program without a report concerning the incident.

I will not hold any of the staff (paid or volunteer) of Grace Arbor responsible for any injury, which occurs to the named participant during the course of the program. I acknowledge that Grace Arbor cannot and does not assume responsibility for undesirable incidents or injuries should the participant leave the program site without permission.

Every reasonable effort will be made to ensure the safety of the participant.

Name: _____ Date: _____

Guardian (relationship)_____ Date: _____

Signature: _____

Participant's Physician Name and Phone #:

_____

Hospital of Choice: _____

NEW PARTICIPANT INFORMATION SHEET

Participant's Name:_____ Start Date:_____

Special Medical or Dietary Alerts:

_____

Special Interests:

Family Information:

_____

Career Information:

Will Be Picked Up By:

_____

GRACE ARBOR

Photo and Field Trip Release

Name: _____ Date: _____

The above mentioned named participant gives permission and release for **Photographs** to be made of him/ her while engaged in program activities. These photos may be used for publicity/ promotion of Grace Arbor and also for identification purposes.

Participant_____ Guardian_____

The above named participant gives permission and release to participate in **Field Trips and Outings** with Grace Arbor. Every effort will be made to insure the safety of the participant.

Participant_____ Guardian_____

GRACE ARBOR

The Congregational Respite Program of
First United Methodist Church of Lawrenceville
395 West Crogan Street
PO Box 2127
Lawrenceville, GA 30046
770-963-0386-Ext. 126
Cell: 678-758-3554

POLICIES AND PROCEDURES MANUAL

Governing Body

The Congregational Respite Program is a ministry under the headship of the Congregational Care Committee of First United Methodist Church of Lawrenceville.

Purpose

Grace Arbor is designed to meet the social, emotional, physical and spiritual needs of adults with dementia and their caregivers. It provides activities and socialization opportunities outside the home in a safe and caring setting for older adults with mild to moderate memory loss and/or medical impairments. It provides their caregivers with emotional support through a caregiver support group, information regarding available resources, and personal time away during the day in which to rest and address their own needs.

Services Offered

For the Adult Participant:

This ministry provides a safe, loving environment for the well-being of each participant. A variety of activities includes, but is not limited to, social, creative, intellectual, spiritual and recreational programming. All activities are designed to provide mental stimulation and social participation. Examples of activities include group singing, gardening, crafts, community services, reminiscing, exercise, adapted floor games, intergenerational programs, art therapy, pet therapy, and socialization activities.

For the Caregiver:

This ministry provides respite (an interval of rest or relief) for the caregiver. It supports the efforts of the family to keep the loved one in the home environment,

which will contribute to the quality of life of the participant as well as the family. This ministry offers a bi-monthly support group with an experienced counselor. It also provides information regarding available community resources, nursing home options, Alzheimer information, etc.

Hours, Days of Operation, Location

Grace Arbor Program operates on Mondays, Tuesdays, Thursdays and Fridays from 10:00 a.m. to 3:00 p.m. in Room 121-123. The program will be closed on all legal holidays, i.e., New Year's Day, Martin Luther King Day, Memorial Day, Fourth of July, Labor Day, Thanksgiving Day and Christmas Day and the week between Christmas and New Years, if they fall on a normal program day, and other holidays that fall on program days. Advanced notification of closing will be communicated to participants and caregivers. If the Gwinnett county schools are closed for inclement weather, we will also be closed.

Admission Criteria

Participation in the program will be based on the applicant's ability to participate in the program and the initial interview with the director. Taken into consideration when evaluating whether an applicant is capable of participating in the program are the following:

- Medical stability-a participant may be frail and have physical problems, but must be medically stable.
- Ability to ambulate independently with or without assistive devices without potential danger to self or others
- Ability to perform daily living activities independently.
- Ability to interact and socialize with others.
- Ability to exhibit acceptable behavior in a group

The following may be examples for excluding an applicant from Grace Arbor:

- Unmanaged incontinence
- Disruptive or combative behavior
- Psychosis
- Communicable disease
- Need for one-on-one continual supervision

Admission Procedure

1. A telephone interview will be conducted by the director, followed by (if potential participant meets criteria) an invitation to visit the program for a day with the participant and caregiver attending. Following assessment an application will be given to the caregiver to be returned to the director.
2. The admission application is processed with a $40 Registration fee.
3. Participant is added to the census and enrolled.

Discharge/Termination Criteria

Examples of reasons for discharging a participant from the program are the same as those listed under Admission Criteria (examples for excluding an applicant section.)

If the caregiver is no longer satisfied with our program or a participant is no longer able to take part in the program due to physical or mental deterioration, the director reserves the right to discontinue the participant from the program. The caregiver will be contacted by phone, e-mail or in person about the need for discharge of the participant. At this time, the director will provide the family with suggestions of program options in the Gwinnett County area that may better serve their needs. Successful placement is not the responsibility of the staff of Grace Arbor.

Discharge/Termination Procedure

Consideration of discharge from the program will be discussed with the family member(s) before final decision of termination is made in order to give as much advance notice as is reasonably possible. Upon the final decision, that discharge will occur and any daily fees paid in advance will be refunded.

Payments/Rates/Attendance

There is a daily fee of $42 per day for participation in the program, which is paid monthly. Statements are issued at the end of the month for the number of days the participant has attended the program. Payment is expected by the 10th of each month in order to ensure uninterrupted participation in the program; any account that remains unpaid after the 10th of the month will incur a $10.00 late fee.

Participants are expected to attend the program as scheduled. Caregivers are asked to notify the director by 9:00 a.m. if the participant will not be in attendance that day. Non-attendance affects both staffing and meal ordering. A $42 fee will be charged on days participant is scheduled to attend, but cancels. Director needs in writing schedule changes.

Staffing

A director and assistant director will staff the program. The director and assistant director are trained in CPR and first aid. In the director's absence the assistant director will be in charge of the operation and activities of Grace Arbor. Trained volunteers provide additional staffing and are assigned participants with whom they will socialize during the day. The ratio of volunteers to participants may vary from 2-4 participants to one volunteer, depending upon individuals. Each program day will be considered "full" when it numbers 23.

Nutrition

A mid-morning snack upon arrival, a nutritious lunch will be served daily. Beverages such as decaffeinated coffee and tea, water and lemonade will be available to participants during the day.

Communication

It is of great importance that lines of communication between caregivers and the program director remain open. If the family of the participant has concerns, observations and/or suggestions they would like to discuss, they are always encouraged to do so. This can be best accomplished by scheduling an appointment with the director.

Medication/Health/Injury

The director will keep a confidential file for each participant, which will include the following:

> Admissions application
> Consent for emergency treatment
> Bill of Rights
> Photo release form
> Current proof of a negative TB test

Participants needing to take medication(s) during program hours must be able to take it/them independently. Participants must keep the medication with them during the day, as we are unable to store medications. Program staff will remind a participant to take his/her medication; however, they are unable to administer any medications. Family members must take full responsibility for medication administration.

No one on staff is a medical professional. If a participant shows signs of illness or infectious disease, the director will contact the participant's caregiver, advising her/him to pick up the participant.

Sickness and accidents resulting in physical injury or suspected physical injury will be reported to the director, who will arrange for appropriate medical attention. The caregiver of the participant will be immediately notified or emergency actions taken. If determined to be necessary, transportation to the hospital will be obtained by calling 911. An accident report will be filed with the signature of the caregiver.

Paid Attendants

Participants may choose to have their personal paid attendant with them during the program hours. Paid assistants will provide necessary aid to their own client, but will be expected to assist their client in participating in the activities as scheduled. They will also be responsible for payment of their own snacks and meals.

Participants' Rights

1. The right to be treated as an adult, with respect and dignity.
2. The right to participate in a program of services and activities that promotes positive attitudes on one's usefulness and capabilities.
3. The right to be free from physical, mental, sexual and verbal abuse, neglect, and exploitation.
4. The right to be free from actual or threatened physical or chemical restraints.
5. The right to be encouraged and supported in maintaining one's independence to the extent that conditions and circumstances permit, and to be involved in a program of services designed to promote personal independence.
6. The right to self-determination within the respite setting, including the opportunity to decide whether or not to participate in any given activity; be involved to the extent possible in program planning and operation; refuse to participate in activities; the right to be cared about in an atmosphere of sincere interest and concern in which needed support and services are provided.
7. The right to privacy and confidentiality.
8. The right to be made aware of the grievance process.

Interviewing the Prospective Caregiver

Knot tying for Shibori Dye Project

Interviewing Prospective Participant's Caregiver

One of the most time-consuming parts of the director's job is the initial interview with a caregiver concerning their loved one and his/her needs. I am going to give you an example of a typical phone call that I receive and how I go through the interview process. As I interview this caregiver, notice the questions that I ask. I want to hear:

- what prompted the caregiver to call me,
- what the physical and mental abilities are of the loved one,
- what health issues besides dementia they are dealing with,
- what their financial need might be, and
- how I can pray for that caregiver at the close of the conversation.

I am a detail person (or try to be!!!). As you interview a caregiver, you must take notes. I have a specific sheet that I record information that the caregiver gives me about the loved one. I fill that in with the details as much as I can, because after I give my information about the program, the caregiver may decide to get back to me. That might take a day, a month, or even six months to a year. If I have a document with their information, I can refer to it when they are ready to visit. If it has been a while, I can ask what has changed since our last conversation. The more detailed you can be, the more professional you come across to the caregiver. I keep all my phone sheets in a folder, recording the date which they called and the date I followed up. Let me say here that the sooner you can follow up, preferably within 24 hours, the better. There may be an extreme need with which you can't help, but you can be a sympathetic ear and a voice used by God to offer comfort and support.

There are many calls you will receive where you cannot help. I try to be sensitive to each need presented but very matter-of-fact about the services we can supply and the condition our participants must be in order to attend our program. The State of Georgia has specific regulations to allow a program to be called a *Congregational Respite* program. My participants must be able to meet those requirements in order to be a part of our program. I make this clear in that initial interview with the caregiver. If I become slack in this area, we could be fined or closed down. Although I am matter-of-fact, I am still sensitive and use listening skills to support the caregiver. *I will put in a plug for Stephen Ministry right now.* This training has been invaluable to me as I direct our program. It has given me the tools to lovingly support a caregiver in time of crisis, to listen, to share words of encouragement, to help, and to pray. If I don't supply any other support than prayer, I feel good about the conversation. Do I feel frustrated when I can't help? YES! I try to provide resources and ideas to share

about what additional help and support might be available to the caregiver. I direct to websites and other agencies if I can. But more than anything, I can share Jesus' love and compassion with the caregiver in this season of his or her life. **NEVER** tell a caregiver or anyone else for that matter that you **"know what they are going through."** You don't nor ever will. Each person is a unique individual with unique life circumstances and experiences. You have no idea what his or her level of coping is or how he/she is truly handling the situation that has resulted in a call to you. Your best response is *"How can I help?"*

Read the following typical conversation I have had with a caregiver who had called me. If the caregiver leaves me a message I will start the conversation with, "Hi, my name is Robin Dill and I direct Grace Arbor. You called earlier today. I am sorry I missed your call. How can I help you?"

This is very short but to the point. I will warn you that these initial calls will take from 20-30 minutes. I try to factor that time into my schedule as I return calls. Often I will return calls from home at night, giving me a chance to unwind from the day, to get dinner, and to be refueled to answer calls. The only drawback to calling from home is that you may not have every resource available to share and may have to make a follow up call the next day.

Phone Conversation:

"Hi, this is Robin."

"Hi, Robin, my name is Susan Smith and I am looking for a daycare for my mother. She has recently moved in with me after my dad died. She really can't live alone so my husband and I moved her up here two months ago from Florida. I thought we would enjoy each other's company and do things together, but she is driving me crazy."

"It sounds like you have had a frustrating time. Susan, I am so sorry about the loss of your dad. Was it sudden?"

"Thanks. He had been sick a while. He was actually caring for mom and I think got burned out. His health declined, and he had a heart attack 2 ½ months ago and died. My sister lived nearby, so she was there to initially help with mom. She works full-time, and it just didn't work."

"Susan, I applaud you for bringing your mom into your home. She is grieving right now and will need lots of support. How old is she, and what is her condition? Why was your dad caring for her?"

"Yeah, my husband and I talked about it and felt that it was the right thing to do. I think it is what my dad would have wanted. I don't work, so I was the best choice of me and my siblings. My mom is 85 and has Alzheimer's disease; she was diagnosed five years ago. She had been doing ok; she was forgetful but able to get around their little town. Dad had to take the car keys away when she kept getting lost going to the grocery store. I think she just wore him out. He could never leave her alone nor would she let dad out of her sight. She went to a program a day or two a week and seemed to enjoy it. I called the Alzheimer's Association and they referred me to you all."

"Susan, what is your mom's physical condition? What is she capable of doing as far as her activities of daily living? And what is her name?"

"My mom's name is Patsy Johnson. She is in good shape. She loves to walk and listen to music. She watches some TV but gets bored. She wants to be around me all the time. I can't even go to the bathroom that she isn't following me!"

"Is she able to toilet on her own? Also does she like other people? The reason I ask this is that we have specific requirements for this program. Our participants must be able to ambulate on their own with or without a cane or walker, feed and toilet themselves, and function in a group setting. According to state rules and regulations, if your mom is on medication and if it needs to be taken during our operating hours, then she must be able to take it on her own. We are not allowed to administer medications because we are not a health model. We can prompt her to take it, however."

"Yeah, Mom can do all that. She used to be a social butterfly. She was in several groups and loved people."

"Has your mom attended a church in her lifetime? The reason I ask is that we are a congregational respite program, a ministry of the church, and we do activities that are faith-based."

"Yeah, mom grew up in the church, and she and dad were very active in their little church in Florida."

At this point in the conversation, I have established that Susan's mother might fit in well at Grace Arbor. I needed, however, to make clear what we offer and what our fees are.

"Susan, let me tell you about our program and how I go about enrolling someone. As I said before, Grace Arbor is a congregational respite program. We minister to people with memory impairment. We offer a very interactive day which keeps them mentally, physically, spiritually, and socially stimulated. We are open from 10AM-3PM Mondays, Tuesdays, Thursdays, and Fridays. We are closed on major holidays and

for the Christmas holidays. We have a social time with a snack in the morning when they come in. This helps the participant make the transition from home to our program. Following this, we move into devotions. During devotional time, we will sing and read a devotional booklet I have created. It contains scripture and questions in it that relate to the topic we will talk about. The questions will be reminiscing-type questions or those pertinent to today. We start and close that time with prayer. After devotions we have our movement time which consists of various arm chair exercises. After movement and blessing of food, we have a bathroom break and lunch. After lunch, depending on the day, we do all kinds of things. Sometimes we have outside entertainment or programs. We might do an art related project, play a mind or active game, or do service project. I try to vary our days according to the calendar.

At this point I may give her an example of what we did yesterday or last week. Most days we end our day with a sing-along. We have fun with that. Many of our folks get up and dance during this time."

"Susan, when someone is interested in our program and I feel they are a match, I invite the caregiver and the potential participant to visit for the day. It gives you a chance to look our program over, and it gives me a chance to assess your loved one. There is no charge for this visit. If it looks good on both ends, I will give you a folder of forms to fill out. We require a TB test and a statement of medical condition from your doctor. When you turn in the paperwork, there is an application fee of $40. The cost for each day your loved one attends is $42. I bill monthly in arrears so you will receive a bill at the end of the first month she attends. Do you have any questions?"

"How many days can she come?"

"She can come all four days we are open, or she may attend three or two days per week."

I have changed my policy to have our participants come at least two days per week. It helps them settle into the routine.

"You set the schedule. We cannot do a drop-in, however. I submit my food count a week ahead of time and we shop for supplies in advance. For these reasons, drop-ins are not possible. If things change and you have doctor visits or appointments, you need to let me know. There is no cost for the days she doesn't come; however, if she is sick, I ask that you call me before 9AM to let me know she isn't coming."

"OK that sounds good. Do you take Medicare?"

"No, we don't. Some long-term health insurance policies pay for daycare. Does she have one? If she does I will be glad to fill out any paperwork to help her get it."

"No, she doesn't have that. I think we could afford two days. We are trying to get dad's estate settled now."

"Susan, we have a scholarship available, if needed. You will have to fill out some forms for that, but we do have a little help there."

"Thanks, but I think we can swing it. When can we come and visit?"

At this point, I check my calendar and schedule an appointment for them to visit. I make sure I have the correct spelling of their names because I will make nametags for them. I also give specific directions to our program.

"Susan, I look forward to meeting you and Patsy next week. Please write down this number in case you need it. It is our cell number, and you may call me in case something comes up that day and you can't make it. It is..... Susan, before we hang up, can I pray for you?"

"Yes! I need all the prayer I can get."

I will pray as the Spirit leads me and close the conversation. Depending on what the caregiver's response is when I ask if the family members go to church may cause me not to pray but to say instead I will be thinking about them or even praying for them. If I get an affirmative response, then I may ask if I can pray right then. You will be amazed at the appreciation a person will give you if you pray. You are inviting Jesus into this crisis situation and giving that caregiver His love and grace. It is powerful!

I hope that by reading through this conversation, you get some ideas of how you will answer the calls you will receive. I don't believe there is any right or wrong way to carry on these conversations, but they do need to be professional, non-judgmental, and supportive. You must be true to your program and true to the church's integrity every time you talk with someone. You are representing Jesus to a hurting person and can give a cup of cold water in the way you respond!

Getting the Word Out

Kentucky Derby Day

We celebrated the Kentucky Derby by creating our own derby hats which we wore during our horse race.

"Getting the Word Out," i.e., Marketing your Program

Once all your planning is done, the volunteers are recruited, and you are ready to begin, the questions comes to mind: "How do I marketing this program?" What are some strategies I can use to let people know that this program will be opening on such and such a date and will be open, let's say, from 10 am to 3pm on Tuesdays and Fridays?"

The first place may seem obvious and is right in front of you: share this with your church! It continues to amaze me how often a church member will tell me they really aren't sure what Grace Arbor is and what it is we do there! When we planned our opening, I spent several Sundays sharing. I spoke at all three worship services. I visited adult Sunday school classes with my brochures to hand out. I mentioned that someone possibly had a neighbor, friend, or a family member who had a need for this program. I visited our circle meetings and let the leaders know the same information. I went to a couple social events with the church to spread the word. I spoke to other weekday ministries within the church in case any of the parents at our preschool or PMO had a need for respite care. Once I exhausted the church, I went outward.

I sent a letter and brochure to all the area churches. In the letter, which our senior pastor wrote, was information about the program and about me as the director. During the following months, I began to contact church leaders, reminding them of our program. I tried to speak at some seniors' events at their churches, but was unsuccessful at the time because I was busy. This would be a great way to get the word out if you have time. Being invited to speak at other churches is a great way to keep the word going out about your respite ministry.

I wrote an article for our Methodist newspaper and submitted it with a picture of our new group. This is sent out to a wide circulation area. I included my contact information in the article.

I invited a reporter from our local paper to do an article about us. Our program was written up in the Georgia Alzheimer's Association's quarterly newsletter.

I visited doctors, senior centers, and any other facility that I felt might deal with older adults with memory impairment. I sent out bundles of brochures to these places so that they were ready to hand out to family members. Keeping these places stocked in the future ensures that they will continue to remember you and share about you.

Networking with others in senior care is vital. We have an organization in Georgia that I think is nationwide called A Place for Mom. I contacted our local representative to share with her about our program. Assisted-living facilities are great contacts because they might refer you. In the future, you may refer them to a family in need.

Don't forget the power of social media. Advertise on Facebook, Instagram, and LinkedIn.

Believe me when I say: TAKE TIME to MARKET!! This is time well-invested and will pay off as the word spreads about your vital ministry!

Safety Issues

Antique Car at Grace Arbor

Safety Issues

Safety is paramount for your program's credibility and longevity. You must, as a director, have eyes everywhere at all times. I can't stress the importance of safety enough! If you pay attention to the details, it will dramatically reduce the number of incidents that may cause falls, illness and closure.

Some of the ideas I will share will deal with everyday issues and what supplies and equipment you need to have on hand. Other ideas will deal with infrequent events, such as a fire drill. As I said previously, pay attention to the details!

Supplies and Equipment:

1. **AED**-this machine, while costly can be the greatest "life saver" in a cardiac emergency. It is very self-explanatory to run, but one must get training. This can be done when you take CPR classes.
2. **First Aid Kit**–check with your local hospital nursing coordinator for tips on how to create a usable kit. It should include gloves, gauze, tape, and Band-Aids.
3. **911 directions for someone to call in case of an emergency**-I have these typed out and on the wall in our program area and outside all bathrooms. It gives simple directions on what to say and where we are exactly located in the church. In the height of an emergency, you may forget details or become confused. These directions are invaluable.
4. **Files on every participant to be kept with you at all times**-these files should contain the family's wishes for which hospital to transport to if 911 is called. This file should have information regarding allergies to drugs and food, a picture of the participant, and any other information that would be vital to the paramedics or you as you care for that person.
5. **Wheel chairs and walkers**–A few extra wheel chairs need to be on hand in case of fire drills or actual fire. They will also be relevant to have on hand if someone becomes weak and can't walk a distance, say to the bathroom.
6. **Extra clothing provided by the family and extra Depends if they wear them**-Toileting accidents are going to occur. Extra clothing will help assist you in preserving the dignity of your participants. Goodwill stores are a great source for extra pants to have on hand. Also keep gloves and wipes in the bathroom.
7. **Clear policy about participants attending when they are ill and what you will do if someone becomes ill during the day**-No one on staff is a medical professional. If a participant shows signs of illness or infectious disease, the director must contact the caregiver, advising her/him to pick up the participant.

You have a responsibility to maintain a safe, healthy environment for all your participants. One sick participant can cause illness to be spread to everyone! Sickness and accidents resulting in physical injury will be responded to by calling 911.

8. **Extra phone numbers to contact family in case of an emergency or illness**–Make sure you have extra phone numbers of someone other than the direct caregiver. I had a situation where I called for 2 hours when a caregiver failed to show up at pick up time. She had given me an alternate number– her cell, but no family or neighbor's number. We had to go to her house and found her asleep!! This was a very scary scenario for us, as well as for the participant. This was a detail I failed to check when I received my paperwork from this family. It was a tough situation for me, but I learned a great lesson!!

9. **Extra sweaters/sweatshirts or shawls**-Without fail, someone will come to your program one day without an extra layer of clothing and become chilly. For their well-being, have some "coverings" on hand to make them feel good.

10. **Boxes of tissues at all times**.

11. **Choking Hazards**–Be aware of any participants who may get "choked" as they eat. People with Alzheimer's disease will sometimes bolt their food. Keep volunteers and yourself aware of who does this and gently remind them to slow down as they eat.

Fire Drills

Fire drills can run smoothly or be one the most hectic things you will accomplish monthly or quarterly. How often you do a fire drill is up to you and your policy at your church or in your state. Here are some helpful hints that will assist you in making it a better experience.

1. Know which participants are able to walk the distance to your "safe spot" and those who can't. For those who cannot, provide a wheelchair or a walker. If a wheelchair is required, remember you will need someone to push that wheelchair. Do not allow another participant to help. Use volunteers or staff to do it.

2. Have ambulatory participants paired with volunteers–one hand holding a volunteer's hand.

3. Designate one person to always be the "lead" person. They will open the door and lead out the group to the safe spot.

4. Some programs use a long rope for everyone to hold onto. I consider this demeaning and could be a safety issue if the rope becomes slack and causes someone to trip and fall.

5. Have a place for all to sit down at your safe spot, such as a picnic table or benches.

6. You as the director need a "Fire Drill Document" that records information about the drill. You will find a copy in the **Form Section**. Take this with you and fill it out on the spot. File it as a permanent record.

7. Take all your files about your participants and a cell phone with you in case of an emergency.

8. You, as the director, will be the last one out the door, having checked the bathrooms and any other places that your participants may be at the time of the drill. When you get outside, take roll to be certain that all are present and accounted for in the "safe spot".

Food Philosophy

Sweet Potato Harvesting

For many years we have participated in a sweet potato project. We read a discussion booklet about sweet potatoes, root the tubers by hanging them in cups of water, observe the potatoes begin to root and vine, and finally plant them in the ground. After approximately 120 days we harvest the potatoes. We bake them and make sweet potato biscuits.

Food Philosophy of Grace Arbor

1. Food should fall under guidelines of nutrition put out by the USDA/AMA. This would include lower fat, lower sodium, and cholesterol.
2. Food should be appealing to all senses–sight, taste, and texture
3. Food should be able to be handled and eaten by older adults who are physically, mentally, and visually challenged. This falls under Georgia State licensure requirements where Congregational Respite participants must be able to feed themselves.
4. The lunch meal has the potential to be our participants' best meal of the day because of the social setting in which it is presented.
5. Food should be balanced with several choices on the plate that will stimulate participants' desire to eat; recognize that older adults with memory impairment present greater challenges with regard to eating than a cognitively sound adult.
6. If you have participants who eat a larger amount as in second portions, plan to have a little extra food each day.
7. Dessert for this group is important. Variety is also important. Pie, cobbler, and cookies (homemade), banana pudding (their favorite) are ideas of choices.
8. Some have participants have dietary restrictions; i.e., sweet potatoes instead of white potatoes, vegetables instead of salad for those with denture issues. If requirements are too difficult to meet, then ask caregivers to pack a lunch for their loved ones.

Programming Ideas and Planning Your Day

Four Season Art Project

Art activities make lovely gifts for family members. One year we made a Four Season apple tree canvas. Our participants painted four quadrants depicting the changes an apple tree goes through in spring, summer, autumn and winter. They chose a scripture which was painted in the section between the seasonal scenes.

Programming Ideas and Planning Your Day

As I began to plan Grace Arbor, I spent time visiting programs around Atlanta to see what they were doing. I asked questions to help me make wise decisions about content and quality. Each Congregational Respite program had some similarities and a lot of differences. I continue to discover that those differences are based on the gifts, talents, and experiences that we directors bring to the table. For example, one program had on staff a professional story teller. She used her gifts to weave stories into the day and the day's topics. Another program had a vivacious director who loved to sing and dance. She had a rousing sing-along at the end of each day. My suggestion to you as you plan your days is to look at your gifts and talents. Look for gifted volunteers to supply aspects of your program where you aren't personally gifted. You do not have to be able to do it all; surrounding yourself with gifted volunteers and support staff will take your program to a new level.

One of the decisions you will need to make up front is the time frame in which your program will be open each day. Remembering that memory-impaired adults can have difficulties "getting going" in the morning as well as "sun-downing" in the afternoon will help you plan your day accordingly. We decided on a five-hour day from 10AM until 3PM. We felt that this fit in with our caregivers' schedules and the traffic demands around Atlanta.

As you plan the day's timeframe, you need to decide what kinds of components you want to bring to your day. Because one of my spiritual gifts is teaching, I plan a written devotional almost daily. I do this in a format in which everyone can participate in reading and sharing in topic-related questions.

Your space area will dictate some of your scheduling times. We are fortunate to have a fenced toddler playground which is on level ground immediately adjacent to our program space. It is actually our entrance. We have utilized some "space sharing" by creating some raised flower beds and other planting areas for different projects. We have grown flowers and vegetables in this shared space. Sweet potatoes are a favorite growing project. We use this space when the weather is optimal for outdoor activities, too. Horseshoe throwing can be an enjoyable activity for your participants when the weather is nice. I believe in purposeful programming. Each activity we do has some kind of cause and effect with the desired result being a joy-filled, meaningful experience

The sweet potato bed was an outgrowth from a discussion booklet done in March. As a group, we learned how to root sweet potatoes and studied their nutritional benefits.

We reminisced about gardening and cooking. After reading the discussion booklet, each participant was given a sweet potato, toothpicks, and a clear cup of water to begin their rooting process. We wrote names on the cups so everyone could keep track of their potato's progress. In a few weeks after the potatoes sprouted vines, the vines were then placed in water and allowed to grow roots. When the vines were fully rooted, we planted them outside in a prepared bed. We are presently watching them grow in the bed. We did an experiment to see whether, if we planted a piece of potato, it would root and grow a vine. In 120 days we will harvest the potatoes and cook with them. One year we made sweet potato biscuits for our Pastor Appreciation luncheon. This is a small example of the meaningful activities you can plan to do. I will share more under the "Activity" section.

The following schedule is what our program has evolved into for a five-hour day. We strive to maintain this schedule for our participants' continuity. Exceptions happen throughout the year but we keep these exceptions to a minimum.

8:30AM Director Setup /Volunteers Arrival

This time is used for set up. We put cloths on tables, placemats, name cards and holders, silverware, and napkins. We decorate the room to make it look like home: quilts on the walls, extra seasonal décor to make the room inviting and fun. We use current art work that our participants have created to add to the décor. After we get everything set up, we take 15-20 minutes to share prayer concerns and pray for our day. The most important thing we do is to ask the Holy Spirit to come and empower us and to be present with us during the day.

10-10:30AM Participants Arrival and Snack

Participants arrive and we gather at the table for conversation and a snack. This time helps our participants transition from home into the day's programming. This is a relaxed, social time.

10:30-10:40 AM Moving into Devotions

Participants and volunteers move from table to chair circle for devotions. Participants are recruited to help pass out hymnals. Volunteers clean up table from snack and set up for lunch.

10:40-11:30AM Devotionals

We begin this time with either prayer or singing. If we begin with singing, the director will pray before we do the actual devotion. Devotions can take many forms. (See section on Activities). After the devotion is over, we might sing another hymn or two and close with prayer. A good transition to the next section is a time for everyone to hug. Another transition is to have everyone tell the person next to them a word or phrase, like: "I'm glad you are here."

11:30AM-12:10PM Movement

Movement can be a combination of exercises and games that stimulate the body and mind. See Activity section for ideas

12:10-12:20PM Bathroom Break and Washing Hands

12:20-1PM Lunch

Plan on this being a relaxing time—not rushed. This may be your participants' best meal of the day.

1-3PM Afternoon Activities

Activities combined with movement and bathroom breaks, as needed. One bathroom break may fall right after lunch before afternoon activities commence.

Afternoon activities offer a lot of creative options. See Activity section for ideas.

Activity Philosophy

Shibori or Indigo Dye Project

Indigo dye is the oldest dye process known to man. We have done this process in several settings. We dyed muslin cloth for scarves, flour sack towels, t-shirts, and tablecloths. This process is exciting to watch because it is a chemical process that occurs when the dye is oxidized.

Activity Philosophy

Quality activity programming takes time. Creativity takes time! The dividends of time invested in planning will pay off as your program expands and grows as a result of your planning. How you plan brings about the uniqueness, desirability, and marketability of your program.

Programming that is meaningful and purposeful should meet the needs and abilities of your participants. Activities should foster enjoyment, engagement, success, and a feeling of accomplishment. Thirty to forty-five minute transitions should be planned for people with dementia to help decrease the opportunity of behavior challenges.

Activities can be changed due to the functioning level of your participants. Higher-functioning participants can handle higher level activities, while those same activities, when presented to lower functioning participants, would result in confusion and possible behavior challenges. Activities can target a group or an individual. All should result in success for the participant.

When an activity fails, look at it as a learning opportunity. Ask yourself, "Why did it fail? What could I have done differently? Were my participants having a bad day? Did I fail in my explanation of the activity?" All these questions will provide valuable planning insight for future activities.

Activities as a Whole

Activities are the "meat and potatoes" of your day. They are what provide the stimulation and enjoyment that cause your participants to want to return to your program. They are what you "do" while you are together. From the minute your participants arrive until the time they go home, they are engaged in activities. Some require intensive planning, like a Veterans Day event. Others are a natural part of the flow of the day, like morning snack. Each activity must be thoughtfully planned out as to how it will fit into your day's schedule.

Some activities will be done as part of your daily routine. Snack and lunch will occur daily. Others will be done less regularly, like a service project or a particular game like "Jeopardy." You will find activities that certain groups love and want to do over and over again. You will find that given a different "mix" of people those activities others loved will not work with your present mix of people. Those activities will be a potential flop. You will not throw them out because you will have a new mix of people to whom you can reintroduce a not-used activity which might be a "hit" at a later date.

My philosophy on activities is to try something at least once, maybe twice. The crazier and "out of the box" type the better. Why? It will potentially be the most stimulating and bring about the most reminiscing of other times in your participants' lives. For example, I do a yearly "apple pie making" day. It is messy, tiring, a little costly, and time-consuming on the set up. I have done it with a small group of five people, as an intergenerational activity with preschoolers and with a large group of 15 participants. Each group has been successful because it is different, physically and emotionally stimulating, and I make it fun. I tell them stories of how my parents had an apple pie day. Then I tell them how my daughter and I spent apple pie days with my dad when mom had dementia. I then ask them about their experiences with baking. This apple pie day has become a tradition and has even turned into a service project because we serve these pies at the Pastor Appreciation Luncheon we do in October to honor the pastors of our church.

On the same note, I tried a winter craft that was a total flop and will never be done again. It was a huge learning experience, however, so it was well worth the flop. It taught me to completely communicate with my volunteers what I need for them to do. It taught me to do a craft in small steps with minimal "stuff" on the table so my participants won't get confused. It taught me to think like one who is memory-impaired as I plan the project to see how far I need to go in my preparation. It reminded me that I really don't like to do crafts!!! But I don't have to if I have a staff member or volunteer who does!!

This activity section will be a culmination of ideas I have gotten from magazines, other publications, brainstorming with staff and volunteers, and from other directors of programs. I am thankful that the Holy Spirit gives me creativity to "run" with an idea and turn it into an activity. I am thankful for fellow activity directors I know who love to brainstorm via texts and emails. We all have the same goal: to provide meaningful activities our participants will enjoy! My prayer for you is that you will yield yourself to His guidance and allow your creative juices to flow!! Don't be afraid to try something. Just do your planning on the front end.

When the activity is over, then evaluate it. If it was successful, ask yourself why. If it flopped, ask yourself how you could have done it differently or was it the mix of people. Through prayer, trial and error, reading, and always seeking, you will develop a fun and interactive program. Activities can fall under a number of categories and can be as creative as time, resources, and the imagination will allow. Just because an activity fails doesn't mean it was time wasted. Continual assessment helps to make a future activity successful. As I said earlier, asking questions (such as "How could I have done this differently? How was my explanation of the activity? Was someone having a bad day?") will help to make future activities more meaningful.

Activities can be structured into the day's programming, which is what I do at Grace Arbor. I have my time slots available as to what might happen during the day and look for activities that will fit that schedule.

Daily to Monthly Activities

Seashell Letter Art Project

This project involved seashells, a 5x7 inch frame that was matted in burlap, paintbrush, and glue. The participants chose seashells, and then glued the seashells onto the burlap in the shape of the first letter in their first name.

Daily to Monthly Activities

I have used "Creative Forecasting Magazine" to help me set "themes" for a certain day or for a particular activity. I have also used the Internet to find unusual or fun days that we could successfully celebrate. I chart my month to the days Grace Arbor will be open and then begin to build activities into the month based on the day's theme. I break my day into components and then begin my planning based on those components. For my program, I know that I will always schedule a devotional/hymn sing time as well as an exercise time. My exercise time may happen one or two times during that day, and it will include body as well as mind exercises. There will be bathroom breaks and meal and snack time. If we have a lot of movement scheduled, I will try to schedule some "downtime" in the form of a discussion book, story sharing, reminiscing about a topic, or outside entertainment.

As I begin to plan based on a theme, I look at resources readily available, consider outside resources if needed, and ask for help from those gifted in a particular area. If someone from another program did a meaningful activity that they will share with me, I will try to "change it up" to fit my program's needs. Our wedding day activity, which includes a renewal of vows ceremony, was modeled after an event by another respite program.

All the time I am considering my participants' level of engaging in the activities and whether or not it will be meaningful. If an activity is strictly geared toward women, I will not consider it on a day that men will attend. We celebrated Lip Appreciation Day with a Mary Kay event with ladies. No men were present that day. How could I have made it an event for both? Possibly turn it into a beauty pageant with men as judges!

As I plan, I have to consider my budget. I also have to consider what resources I have to purchase or what paid entertainment I have to plan for each month. As I plan, I need to be aware of people who might be able to donate something or volunteer their time to help with an activity.

My goals for each day are these:

1. To honor and glorify God
2. To provide love, acceptance, and joy to the participants
3. To provide a service opportunity for the volunteers of the church and community to use their gifts and talents at Grace Arbor
4. To provide opportunities for the participants to feel accepted, purposeful, independent and successful, and to laugh

Example:

National Pickle Day:

1. I created a devotional that tied into that theme (believe it or not) I did this in the form of a discussion booklet in which the participants can read and share answers to questions related to the devotion.

2. As a group we made Reuben sandwiches (Sauerkraut is a pickled cabbage) I purchased rye bread, sauerkraut, Swiss cheese, Thousand Island dressing and pastrami. I had an electric skillet to grill the sandwiches. We made the sandwiches in an "assembly line" with someone getting two pieces of bread, another putting the dressing on the bread, another cheese, another the pastrami, another the sauerkraut, and the last person putting the top slice with margarine. My highest-functioning person helped me "grill" and the lowest helped a volunteer set the table. The whole time we are doing this we are sharing about times we have made lunch for others, what our favorite kind of sandwich is, etc. This was a movement activity because most stood and worked on the assembly line.

3. I created a discussion book about pickles by going on the National Pickle website and downloading information. We had a circle discussion about pickles, and it led up to our pickle-making activity. It gave us an opportunity to have "down" time and enjoy sharing about pickles and laughing at the crazy things you could make with them!

4. We made pickles by slicing cucumbers, creating our "sauce," and mixing them together, and putting them in storage containers. There was a safety factor to consider when I planned this activity. We used serrated knives to slice the cucumbers. I considered who was able to use one before we began. If someone couldn't use a knife, then they were given other jobs to do such as washing the cucumbers, mixing the spices and the vinegar together; and spooning the "pickles" into the containers.

This was a highly successful day and one I wrote an article about that went into the church newsletter. After all, when one's last name is *Dill,* it is imperative that we salute National Pickle Day!

Looking at the Year Ahead

Four Season Group Project

This project stretches for four days as we paint, as a group, an outdoor scene that changes with the seasons. We hang these canvases up in our program room. They remind us that even though the seasons change, God's love is constant.

Looking at the Year Ahead

As you settle into planning your months' themes and activities, you will be able to think ahead for an entire year. Is it an Olympic year? Plan a summer or winter Olympics at your program. Creatively think of sports that would fit under the venues you plan. When we celebrate the Winter Olympics, our Ladies Figure Skating consists of a rhythmic interpretation of music as they are driven in a wheel chair with ribbon sticks in their hands. Our men are the judges who have been given number cards to hold up. We give medals after each venue with the National Anthem being played. We use this as a cultural experience as well. This year, with the summer Olympics in Rio, we learned about Brazil, ate food from Rio, and danced to a Salsa Band!

I have planned our year's calendar to have a couple months to be heavier on art projects. March is a month where we create, look at, or welcome local artists every day we are open. October is the month we typically create a group art project. July is a month that most music teachers are on summer break so we celebrate music that month. This is an intensively detailed scheduling event but has been one of huge blessings. Celebrating different instruments of the orchestra and vocal presentations plus hearing about the musicians' stories have proven highly successful and stimulating!

How does your schedule compare to how religious and other holidays land? Last year I used an Advent devotional that was currently in print for our devotions during December. I gave a copy to each of my volunteers and participant families as a gift. Speaking of December, are you open during Hanukkah? This might be a fun day to learn of the food, stories, and games associated with this Jewish Holiday.

Summertime can be a time to integrate the youth of your congregation in your program. You might plan an intergenerational dance or specific activities to combine the talents of your youth to interact with the interests of your participants.

For a more detailed description of specific activities or questions, please email me at rdill@fumclv.org.

Spiritual Activities

Renewal of Marriage Vows Wedding Week

One of the most poignant activities we do is our renewal of vows ceremony. We ask a couple, with a loved one in the program, to renew their covenant of marriage. Family and friends are invited, special music is played, vows are exchanged with our minister of Congregational Care, and a reception with cake and punch is shared.

Spiritual Activities

One of my spiritual gifts is teaching. I have been a Sunday school teacher, neighborhood Bible study leader, and a lover of God's Word for many years. Spiritual activities stimulate me because they provide an avenue to share my love of Jesus Christ and His word in creative ways. I use many resources during my devotional times. I try to change things up so we don't get into a rut, and it stays fresh and stimulating for my volunteers. We do spiritual activities daily for several reasons:

1. Most of our participants are no longer attending weekly worship services.
2. Spiritual activities bring out the truths that were sown into hearts and minds a long time ago. Most of our participants grew up going to church. Singing and reading Bible stories is what they were used to doing when they were younger.
3. Opportunities for sharing and healing happen during our devotional times. I will never forget the time that we were doing a devotion on a topic that had to do with loss, and one of our participants shared about his young son's death and how it led him to become an alcoholic and how Jesus set him free. It was a powerful testimony that came about because of God's word being opened and shared.
4. Daily devotions bring unity and love into our circle. We have many denominations represented in our groups. We learn about our differences and similarities. We always end our time with some demonstration of love–a hug or a hand shake. It truly sets the tone for the rest of the day.

Our spiritual activities take approximately 45 minutes. We begin with prayer, move on to singing two to three hymns, share the Word in some form or another, perhaps sing a few more hymns, and end with prayer. I try to give a direct verbal signal to begin and end our devotional time so that they know we have transitioned into and are transitioning out of this time. We stay in the same spot after devotions most days and do our morning exercises. Verbally transitioning helps cue them for another activity. Some days when we end our devotion time with a "hug three people" that is the verbal cue. One of my participants brought the importance of this action to me, so I try to do this daily.

Spiritual Activity Equipment and Resources

1. **1 ½ inch binder with large print hymns in non-glare plastic sleeves**. I copy hymns at 125% for large print. I put stickers on the bottom right-hand side with the page number. A table of contents is at the front of the book with page numbers so people can look at a list and pick a favorite hymn.

2. **A calendar** that has different Jewish and Christian holidays identified throughout the year. Having a calendar with Holy days is a way of incorporating different ideas into your devotionals. I try to do a devotional booklet about each of the Jewish holidays. It is interesting and helps them understand their heritage.

3. **Various *Chicken Soup for the Soul* books or *Stories for the Heart* books.** I use these books all the time as an extra part of my devotional time. I will pick a topic for a devotional and then look through my books to see if I can find a story that goes along with my devotional. My participants love to hear stories.

4. **Children's Picture Books.** Every fall and Christmas, I pull out several children's books to share with my group for devotions. I use a beautiful book when I share about St Francis of Assisi. I share a Stephen Kellogg book when I talk about the life of John Chapman (Johnny Appleseed). I share at least one children's Christmas book a day during Advent because the wording, message, and illustrations are pleasing and easily understood. I try when I introduce the books to not make the hearers feel like they are being treated like children, but I let them know that the particular book I am about to share says it best!

5. **The Message Bible along with your favorite translation of the Bible.** When I create devotional booklets, I use the Message Bible the most as the translation in the booklet. It is written in language that is easily understood and is a fresh presentation. If I create a booklet that has a familiar Psalm like Psalm 23 I will use the King James translation because it is what the participants will remember.

6. **The book, *Full Circle, Spiritual Therapy for the Elderly* by Kevin Kirkland and Howard McIlveen.** This is a valuable resource for your program and devotional time. It has great topical ideas, scriptures, and hymns and songs.

7. **A piano and piano player with someone to lead the singing.** You may not be a singer but you can recruit a volunteer to lead the singing part of devotions. Hymns can be sung acapella or to CDs as well.

8. **Props if you are going to "act out" a scripture.** I rewrote the Good Samaritan in a modern-day version and we act it out. It has become a favorite of ours to do.

Spiritual Activity Ideas

1. **Devotional Booklets.** This is a concept that I learned from Dr. Cameron Camp's program: *Montessori Method for Dementia Patients*. I create booklets that include topical questions, in addition to a scripture that is based on a theme. See example. We begin by discussing the cover artwork–exploring the message behind the picture. I choose my "readers" from the participants and if I need extras then I use the volunteers. I will have a participant read one page and if there is a question I ask them to pause after the question. If we spend a lot of time on the question I will redirect the participant who is reading to where we stopped prior to the question. Some ideas I have used for devotions come from a favorite scripture, what is going on in the calendar, and the season of the year we are in. On the first day of Fall, I do a devotion on "Change." During Holy Week, we do a devotion on "Saying Goodbye." Visual props brought in during this time are very effective.

2. **Scripture turned into a play or interactive reading.** As mentioned previously I rewrote the story of the Good Samaritan in modern language and we act it out. Interactive reading can be done through everyone reading together a Psalm aloud.

3. **Communion.** Twice a month we have a Communion service. I utilize retired ministers as well as the ministers on staff at our church to conduct the liturgy. The format is printed in large print (20-22 Arial font).

4. **Brainstorming and Writing Prayers and Psalms.** We love to brainstorm as a group. This is an effective mind activity which can turn into a spiritual activity. Our group has written a Psalm of praise in response to a devotion. We have written prayers that have been used as gifts. We have taken words and brainstormed acrostic poems. See Harvest Blessings on the next page. We brainstormed this acrostic then turned it into a poem for a non-profit clinic which is located next door to our church. We presented this to the clinic as a gift. We framed it and also made bookmarks with the poem for the staff.

5. **Celebrating Holy Days.** We celebrate several Holy Days in our program. The most time-intensive is our Seder meal which we celebrate on Maundy Thursday. This is a whole-day activity with many components. Some of the other days we celebrate are Thanksgiving, Christmas, Easter, Marriage, Rosh Hashanah, Yom Kippur, Hanukah, Purim.

H elping the needy,

A ssisting the poor,

R ecovery bringing,

V olunteers galore!

E nergetic staff,

S incere in love,

T rustworthy and honest,

B eneficial results from above.

L oving the patients,

E xcellent in care,

S uperior in giving,

S upporting everywhere.

I ntelligent thinking,

N urturing of man,

G odly in spirit,

S erving with helping hands.

Art Activities

Bluebird Box Activity

Everyone desires to find purpose in their life, even people dealing with memory issues. Our bluebird box project has been in existence for nine years. With the assistance of some very hardworking wood workers, we paint and stain the fronts and boxes as a service project for the Hope Clinic, a not for profit local medical clinic. It is a way for our folks to use their talents to help others!

Art Activities

When I think of art activities, I think of creativity and exploration. Art has a way of making connections with people with dementia in much the same way as music. There are deep connections that happen, but unlike with music, they may need to be nurtured and encouraged. Art activities take time: on the front end, during, and at the back end.

Planning is critical. Planning must process how a person with dementia goes through the activity, and adding the necessary time and steps needed for success. Art with people with dementia should never be like art with children who progress in their abilities. **It will never be "perfect" but it will be theirs.** Sending home a beautiful piece of art should not be your goal. Sending home a piece where your participant found enjoyment in the exploration is your goal. That being said, guiding someone in an activity and sometimes guiding their hands is ok. Doing an activity for them is **not**.

Where are my sources for art? My greatest sources have been trainings, Pinterest, articles online, and ideas from other directors. Learning the process of taking a person with dementia through an art experience is invaluable. Understanding how their brains work, what their visual field is doing, and taking the time to let the process happen is so important. Your setting is equally important. A quiet place, where a person who is already struggling with the ability to concentrate, is crucial. The question of background music always comes up. Unless your art project includes a response to that background music I would say do not use it. A lot of conversation is also detrimental. They need quiet and space to explore.

As you look at projects, on Pinterest for example, break them down into steps. Do not put all your supplies out at once. Whatever you need for that step, put out. When the next step is ready to begin, add the supplies. This helps decrease confusion and too much stuff in your work space. The simpler, the better.

Art can be presented in a demonstration, as in someone throwing a pot on a wheel; exploration, as in an MOMA experience; or a hands-on creating project. Each can be stimulating. Inviting artists to come and share some of their work and talk about their love of art can be quite exciting. Hearing their passion and reasons for creating can help propel you all into trying a project of your own. For example, invite a watercolor artist to share his or her work and then take your folks through a watercolor experience.

One of my favorite demonstration/individual projects is Shibori dyeing. Indigo is the oldest dye on the planet, and the process is fascinating to observe because it happens

through oxidation. You can order this dye on Amazon. It gives you a list of supplies you will need (two large plastic 5-gallon buckets with lids) plus the type of fabric, etc. We have done this project with t-shirts, muslin, and tablecloths.

As you gather supplies for art, do not scrimp on cost. High-quality products last longer and make your participants feel like grownups rather than children. Buy good quality watercolor palettes, like Prang instead of Crayola. There are art distributors, like Blick, who offer sales and discounts.

Paper quality is important, especially when doing watercolor projects. Do not use regular drawing paper as it will pill and breakdown easily.

A sister program has spent the money to go through OMA training. Opening Minds Through Art (OMA) is an intergenerational art program based at the Scripps Gerontology Center, an Ohio Center of Excellence at Miami University, and is tailored for people living with neurocognitive disorders including memory loss. The program is aimed at promoting the social engagement, autonomy, and dignity of people with memory loss through creative self-expression. OMA is designed to show that a person living with memory loss has a unique self that can be expressed through art. You may want to explore this approach, but realize it is expensive.

At Grace Arbor, March is designated as our art-focus month. Every day we have an art-related activity. We will create, be visited by an artist, or explore art as an MOMA activity. At the end of the month we have an art show where their art is displayed in a gallery type setting. I set up spaces in our program area where each type of work is displayed. During the art show a short demonstration is done to explain the process we went through to create that particular project. For some of our folks with dementia, seeing this gallery will be like exploring the project for the first time! After the show, the art goes home.

One of my favorite activities in March is learning about a master artist, for example Monet or Louise Nevelson, and then recreating their art work. When we study Louise Nevelson, we take three to four days. On the first day, we learn about her life and work in the form of a discussion booklet that I have written. On the second day we do a group project (our program will split into groups of five to seven people) where we build a wooden structure. The third and/or fourth day, the groups paint their structures and name them. They will be showcased in an art show at the end of the month.

Supplies:

Small containers and paper or plastic plates for palettes

Brushes: both for acrylics and watercolors; foam brushes for wood projects

Paper: watercolor, drawing, canvas paper

Various size canvas for painting projects

Acrylic paints: I use tubes for canvases and bottles for wood projects

Watercolor palettes

Pastels and oil pastels

Black construction paper or card stock for mattes

Plastic aprons and gloves

Wood: scraps for building structures, birdhouses or any other paintable project

Metal cart

For specific ideas email me at rdill@fumclv.

Musical Activities

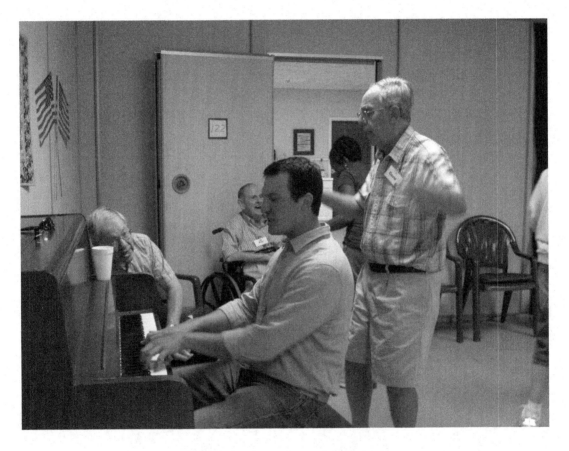

Kevin and the Guys Sing-along

We close each day with a sing-along activity. Usually a piano player or guitar player leads the music. Singing, dancing, and fun are the purpose of this beloved time!

Musical Activities

Music is a huge part of my program. I have discovered that music touches people with memory impairment deeper than anything else. A song or hymn will bring up a feeling, a memory, or words when a person can't even speak a sentence. Song lyrics will be recalled even when thoughts can no longer can be spoken!

Musical activities can stand alone or be incorporated into other activities such as devotions or exercise. They can be planned out in a discussion book about a famous musician, incorporating a CD of his/her music as a part of the afternoon sing-along.

Musical activities can be intergenerational when songs such as camp songs or typical children's songs are shared. "If You're Happy and You Know It" and the "Hokey Pokey" are examples of intergenerational songs. Inviting children to join you in your musical time can be a fulfilling experience for both your participants as well as the children. It can foster joy and relationships.

Exploring musical instruments can also be a meaningful intergenerational music activity. We have used choir chimes and recently purchased choir chimettes from Suzuki to play in a group setting. Each participant plays a chime while the director points to him/her when it is his/her time to ring. Creating music, corporately, has a magical effect on people. They are amazed that they can make music, together, that is beautiful. This is one of our most loved activities!

Musical activities can be part of your "outside" programming. Watch your local paper or ask around the church for different musicians who might be able to perform for your program. The activity can be as simple as a solo instrumentalist, barbershop quartet, swing band, or high school music students. You can plan a "dance" around a swing band's performance. Advertise, invite your congregation, have some simple refreshments and decorations, and you have the makings of a fun time!

July is a wonderful month to focus on music in your program because most teachers and students are out of school. Create a month where your participants meet the orchestra or band. Invite a teacher or student each day to talk about and play his/her particular instrument or instrument family. Perhaps you could end this month's experience by having a concert given by an ensemble.

A fellow respite director's program has created a "Side-by-Side" choir where participants and their caregivers participate in a formal singing experience under the direction of a choir director. What started as a time of joy and shared experience has become a monthly concert at a local museum!

Your calendar might declare a certain month as National Piano Month (September). I try to invite certain musicians during these "specific" months to add depth to my programming. It requires planning ahead, but is very doable if you are organized!

I have located performers on the Internet and by word of mouth. Other programs in my area try to share ideas, so keep your ears and eyes open. I am always looking for someone or something to entertain our participants.

However you choose to implement music in your program, do it! Music makes connections where the spoken word can fail. You will be blessed by your efforts!

Taking Care of Your Caregivers

Caregiver Support Group

Caring for our caregivers takes many forms. One is our caregiver support group which meets every other week throughout the year. Our group is led by a Stephen minister.

Taking Care of Your Caregivers

By now, after interviewing some caregivers and hearing their stories, you are getting a picture of the life of stress they lead. I believe our respite ministry can be a haven for our caregivers on many levels:

1. ***It is a safe place for their loved ones to spend a five-hour day.*** After a family visits our program, I conduct a follow-up call with the caregiver. Most of the time I will hear words that affirm what we are doing, how much they enjoyed the atmosphere of the ministry, and how welcome they felt. They will often express that they wish they could attend it! There was a time, when we first started, that I wanted each visit to be "perfect." I wanted no behavior issues, no safety concerns, and all to run smoothly. Well, along about month three, we had our first Veterans' celebration and had a family visiting. One of our participants had a seizure and became unresponsive. Our visitors saw us in action that day and realized that this would be a safe place for their loved ones to spend the day.

2. ***It is a place where the caregiver is supported.*** Many days I can gauge how a caregiver is doing by their tone of voice, their interaction with their loved one, or their body language. It is at the beginning of the day, as our participants are coming in or at the end of the day as they are leaving that great, supportive ministry can happen. That ministry can take the form of a long hug, a listening ear, a pull aside for a prayer, or a promised follow-up call that night. You may be the only person a caregiver feels comfortable to talk to about their concerns. I find that men caring for their wives need a special type of care: compassionate and yet very direct. Some of our male caregivers struggle with the bathroom aspect of their wife's care. Being honest and direct is much better than being vague. You can be that place of information and support.

3. ***It is a place of God's presence that reflects peace to our caregivers.*** Having a place where caregivers can "breathe in" and receive peace is vitally important. Having a caregiver support group goes hand-in-hand with this concept. Caregivers need a place to vent and share ideas. A support group, led by a trained, loving Stephen minister or professional is vital to your ministry. Listening and reflecting and ultimately pointing them to God in loving communion with other caregivers are needed. Our caregiver support group has a group of former caregivers as a part of it. These champions, who have already completed their race with their loved ones, have chosen to walk alongside present caregivers to encourage and offer wisdom and insight. It is an absolutely beautiful experience to see in action!

4. ***It is a place of knowledge sharing***. Caregiver classes, coupled with a support group, means better-equipped caregivers. Knowledge is power. Helping your caregivers understand the disease process, helping them to better handle difficult behaviors, and even how to take care of themselves can be powerful. We began with the training, *Powerful Tools for Caregivers*. This is a national, scripted program that takes caregivers through a course designed to give caregivers tools for caregiving. Communication techniques, how to take care of yourself by dealing with stress, and developing a weekly action plan are some examples of the tools. After offering the scripted program several times, my teaching partner and I decided to branch out to offer other knowledge areas our caregivers needed: hospice, finances, end-of-life celebration and burial, and pharmaceuticals, to name a few. These "classes" are offered on an as-needed basis in the time frame of six to eight weeks, with each session being two hours. We have offered these classes opposite the caregiver support group so that our caregivers don't miss that bimonthly support.

5. ***Finally it is a place of security***. You will probably be the one your caregivers will turn to in *times* of crisis after the family is contacted. You will be a source of much-needed resources for the caregiver. Taking the time to educate yourself concerning local, state, and national resources will help you as you journey with families in crisis. Many of the telephone calls I receive are about sharing resources. As you come alongside the caregivers of the participants in your program, you will develop a level of trust and care that will possibly bring about a lasting friendship. Our caregivers have called in times of need and have asked me to speak at their loved ones' funerals. I have walked a tough journey with them and count it a supreme honor to be there with them on this journey!

Resource Guide

Kevin and Darrell Hyde

One of the greatest resources you can have is a list of musicians. These artists will create connections with your participants that no one else is able to do. The above picture is of the late Darrell Hyde and his son, Kevin. Darrell answered an ad in our church's newsletter that I placed concerning the need for a Friday musician for our sing-along time. He told me that his son, Kevin, was a professional musician and perhaps they could serve together. Serve they did, in fact, they served two days a week for six years!

Resource Guide

1. "Creative Forecasting"
   a. PO Box 7789, Colorado Springs, CO 80933
   b. 719-633-3174
   Monthly publication for activity and professionals.

2. *Full Circle, Spiritual Therapy for the Elderly* by Kevin Kirkland and Howard McIlveen.
3. *Montessori-Based Activities for Persons with Dementia Volume 1&2* by Cameron J. Camp, Ph.D. Editor
4. *Positive Interactions Program of Activities for People with Alzheimer's Disease* by Sylvia Nissenboim and Christine Vroman
5. *Alzheimer's Disease Activity-Focused Care* by Carly R. Hellen
6. *Chicken Soup for the Soul* books
7. *Stories for the Heart* and *More Stories for the Heart* compiled by Alice Gray
8. Grosfillex Furniture Company
   a. 230 Old West Penn Ave., Robesonia, PA 19551
   b. 610-693-5835
   www.grosfillexfurniture.com

9. Dallas Midwest Office Furniture
   4100 Alpha Rd, Dallas, TX 75244
   1-800-527-2417

10. Pinterest
    a. Great source for art, craft, games, and gift ideas

11. *Then Sings My Soul* by Robert J. Morgan
12. Exercise: A Video from the National Institute on Aging
    a. This is a great catalog to order activity equipment. We ordered our bowling, shuffleboard, and other game supplies from this company

13. Wolverine Sports Catalog 800-521-283
14. *The Four Things that Matter Most* by Ira Brock, M.D.
15. *End of Life: Helping with Comfort and Care* from National Institute on Aging
16. *Seasons of Caring* by Clergy Against Alzheimer's

Websites:

Alzheimer's Association: www.alz.org

National Coalition on Aging: www.ncoa.org/

National Hispanic Council on Aging: www.nhcoa.org

National Alliance on Caregiving: www.caregiving.org

Free Crossword and other puzzle-making site: www.puzzle-maker.com

Center for Applied Research in Dementia:

This is the training site for Montessori-type dementia resources and Dr. Cameron Camp

www.cen4ard.com

National Institute on Aging:

Great exercise video and other resources

www.nia.nih.gov

ARCH National Respite Network: www.archrespite.org

Teepa Snow:

Positive Approach to Brain Change

www.teepasnow.com

The Senior Gems DVD

Produced by Senior Helpers and Teepa Snow

available at seniorhelpers.com

Dick Blick Art Supply

www.dickblick.com

Printed in the United States
By Bookmasters